# Helen And Her Brothers

James W. White

Cover photo courtesy of Government of Western Australia, WA Museum Collections and Research
ISBN: 978-93-95131-07-0

First Edition: 2023
Rs. 200/-

**_ROCHAK PUBLISHING_**
HIG 45 Kaushambi Kunj, Kalindipuram
Allahabad - 211011 (U.P.) India
https://rochakpublishing.com/
Tel: +(91) 9415091004
E-mail: info@rochakpublishing.com



Printed at VCORE CONNECT LLP.

**For Anita McCall**

## COVER ART ACKNEWLEDGEMENT

Cover art photographer, Vintage Images, “1930s 1940s Two Teen Boys One Girl,” 2022, via https://vintage-images.pixels.com/featured/1930s-1940s-two-teen-boys-one-girl-vintage-images.html

Cover art design courtesy of Becky Bishop White

# Contents

# Chapter 1

Helen slouched in her favorite chair, leaned back and kicked off her shoes. Gazing out the front window that framed a stately line of mature sycamore trees, she took a deep breath and let it out slowly. Her best friend and roommate, Jessie Mae, was busy unpacking in their shared bedroom after a week-long family visit to Dallas. Their apartment was small enough Helen didn't have to raise her voice to be heard. "We put poor old Grandfather away Sunday afternoon," she said, sitting up and reaching for a tall glass of lemonade on a side table next to her chair. Ice chips tinkled as she brought the glass to her lips. It was a warm, Texas afternoon in August, Friday, 1936.

After a moment of silence followed by the rasping sound of a drawer closing, Jessie Mae stuck her head out the bedroom door. "So I heard. Mama told me the whole Steves clan was there."

Helen took another sip of lemonade and savored the cold, flavorful sensation. "Yeah, the service was at the gravesite. It was a simple affair."

"How'd he look?"

Helen was quiet for a minute. She stretched her legs and wiggled her toes. "He was absolutely beautiful, Jessie. Everybody said so." A horse-drawn delivery wagon stopped in front of the grocery store downstairs from their apartment. The horse's bell jingled the wagon's arrival. "His suit was dark gray and looked perfect. His casket was a lovely gray. Nothing black."

"He was sick a long time before he died, right?"

"Yes, and he looked pale, very pale, but there wasn't a wrinkle on his face. His features were as pure and clear as marble. Honest, Jessie,

I was so proud of him. He looked like an aristocrat, and I don't mean maybe."

A clatter came from downstairs as the deliveryman hauled crates of produce from his wagon into the store. Helen smiled. The noise made her appreciate her day off.

Jessie Mae walked into the living room with her own glass of lemonade, carrying a small, wrapped package in her free hand. "I brought you a souvenir from Dallas."

"Fer me? Oh, Messy Jay, you shouldn't have done that." Helen set her glass on the table, accepted the proffered package, and pulled on a red ribbon. "And such a pretty bow. You're so sweet."

"I was thinking about you going to your granddad's funeral all the while I was sashaying around the big D and I felt sorry for you. So I got a little something to cheer you up."

Helen handed Jessie Mae the colored paper while she unwrapped. "It was a big crowd. Eugene Meeks led the singing and there were lots of flowers." She held up a small vial of perfume to the light coming from the parlor window. "Shalimar! How'd ya know that's my favorite!"

Jessie Mae smiled. "I saw an empty spray bottle in your dresser, that's how."

"I love your thoughtful self so much." Helen raised an eyebrow. "So long as you don't snoop around my stuff." She opened the vial and motioned Jessie Mae to come close. She dabbed a finger of perfume on Jessie Mae's neck then one on hers. "There now, we're both irresistible."

Jessie Mae rolled her eyes and folded the wrapping paper. "So, go on about the funeral. I want to hear the full story. What about music?"

Helen stood and waltzed in the cramped space of their living room clutching the vial to her chest. "One Two Three, One Two Three. The first song was 'Unclouded Day,' one of Grandfather's favorites. It was so pretty I could hardly stand it. Then they sang 'In The Land Where We'll Never Grow Old' and later 'Shall We Gather At The River,' 'Sweet Bye and Bye' and 'Rock of Ages.'"

"Five songs?" Jessie Mae's eyes went wide. "And you call that simple? Well, I never."

"Well, it was," Helen nodded. She set the vial on a bookshelf and dropped back into her chair with a gasp. "Reverend Renfro, a friend of Grandfather's from Goldthwaite, led the service. His talk was about finding meaning in your life through those who love you. And Reverend Cooper led the closing prayer."

Jessie Mae adjusted a painting that hung crooked on the wall next to the kitchen door on her way into kitchen. "Where was your mother all this time?"

"Mama and me sat with Lizzie Garrett Lovelace." Helen twisted in her chair to face the kitchen, one leg tucked under her. "We got to talking after the burial and Lizzie told me I looked so much like Mama. I said 'Thanks, I always wanted to.' Then Lizzie said, 'I don't blame you, so did I, but I never could.' Mama blushed, and we all laughed."

Jessie Mae chuckled from the kitchen. "So that's where you get your good looks. I take it Preston's troth is on account of your Mama and Shalimar –"

"Oh, you shush," Helen giggled. "Preston doesn't know Shalimar from Shinola. Anyways, speaking of boys, a lot of people asked about 'em."

"I'm sure they did. Have you heard from them?"

"Not a peep." Helen bit her lip and frowned. "But I'm not surprised," she quickly added. "California must be a big distraction for those two, er... three, I mean."

Jessie Mae stuck her head out the kitchen door. “Oh yeah, I forgot about your cousin Sam. He’s there too.”

“Sure enough is.” Helen got up from the chair and from the front window, watched the produce wagon move down the street at a leisurely pace. “He’s the reason Robert wanted to go out there in the first place.”

“Strange boy, Sam.” Jessie Mae said. “I kinda liked him when we were in school, but he was cold as a fish. Know what I mean?”

Helen nodded absentmindedly, picking up her lemonade and remembering her school days. Jessie Mae was right. Sam wasn’t like the other boys. Same as her older brother Robert. The two of them had things in common, like being quiet and unpopular. “He was Robert’s best and, far as I know, his only true friend,” she said. “Still is, I suppose.”

“Two of a kind,” Jessie Mae replied.

The view beyond the street melded into an unfocused tableau of green and brown as Helen imagined her brothers in California, walking amid crowds of colorful people, the ocean, the tall buildings and fancy stores and movie stars. It seemed a magical place. She wondered if she would like to live there. The idea seemed both exciting and intimidating.

An automobile backfired while passing in front of their building, snapping Helen out of her reverie. It was quiet in the kitchen, with an occasional clatter of plates and utensils.

Helen turned from the window that led to California and picked up Preston McClain’s framed photograph that sat on the sideboard. *I’m incorrigible*, she thought. *Always looking for what is not.* She gently caressed Preston’s face with her finger. She had surprised herself how quickly she responded to his shy, modest overtures, almost two years ago under the shade of a locust tree during the Spring Break picnic. Despite his handicap, he was friendly and courteous, and that had caught Helen’s eye. She had enjoyed encouraging him to overcome his insecurities, but his unwillingness to improve left Helen frustrated. He refused to dance, rarely had a drink, and was completely dependent on Helen to arrange their social lives.

His unstylish longish blond hair and sorrowful eyes, hidden behind rimless glasses, made Preston one of Brownwood High's social outcasts. Some were deficient in mental, physical, or social development, others simply refused to participate with the in-crowd's tiresome games of competitive adulation. Preston was a combination of both. Born with a congenital heart condition, he avoided strenuous sports and social engagements. Prodded by his parents, he often made an appearance, but always as a solitary bystander. He preferred to watch rather than suffer the ignominy of rejection that would surely follow if he tried to participate.

When Helen discovered the poor lost puppy, she appraised him to be damaged, but salvageable. During the senior spring picnic, she had asked Preston to be her date. It wasn't love at first sight, but Preston's genuinely eager acceptance tugged at Helen's heart. "You're fine," she'd told him when, by way of introduction, he apologized to her about his heart condition. "Don't be such a sissy," she'd admonished him when he hesitated to participate with her in the three-legged race. "Attaboy!" she'd whooped when the two of them charged across the finish line, not the first, but not the last either. From that day on, he cautiously stepped out of his protective shell so long as Helen was close by his side.

Noise from the kitchen interrupted Helen's thoughts. She set the photograph down and shook her head to forget the memory. *Are there nice guys in California*? she wondered. "What you doin' in there?" she said.

"Makin' lunch. Want some?"

* * *

Ruth clutched the railing while Helen escorted her mother up the stairs to her apartment. Helen hummed a popular tune, 'Ain't She Sweet' that was playing on the radio day and night. Their weekly coffee social, as they called it, alternated between Ruth's and Helen's apartments. "You sound as chipper as a tornado in an auto camp," Ruth said, stopping at the top of the stairs to catch her breath. "I hardly have enough breath to wheeze, much less hum a tune."

It was another warm day and Helen had left the windows open. A breeze passed through the apartment bringing scents of fresh mowed grass, blossoms, and newly tilled earth. Ruth quickly found her favorite place to sit and let go with a sigh.

"Oh Mama," Helen moved to the kitchen, "don't be so dramatic. You're as strong as an ox."

Ruth shook her head. "Oxen have other characteristics I'd rather not be associated with. Where's Jessie Mae?"

Helen coughed. "At work, I reckon. We're all by our lonesome." She rubbed her throat. "I'm getting a sore throat," she added. "I've been sucking on cough drops like they're candy."

Ruth stood and with a low groan she followed Helen into the kitchen. She felt her daughter's forehead and the side of her neck. "Let me have a look at your throat. You're not feverish."

Helen backed away. "It's nothing, Mama. Not a cold or anything like that. Didn't you tell me I had my tonsils taken out when I was five?"

Ruth considered the question for a moment. "Yes. I remember you had them taken out the summer you turned five. Doctor had you eating ice cream for two weeks."

"Maybe I'm allergic. It's hay fever season," Helen said while she arranged the coffee serving. "I feel fine otherwise."

"Squeeze a lemon in hot water," Ruth suggested. "Plus a spoonful of honey." Returning to the living room, she took a handkerchief from her purse and wiped the chair's armrest before she sat back down. "Speaking of lonesome, it sure seems lonesome without our baby to tend to, but I'm glad he's out of his misery."

Helen placed the tray on the coffee table. She raised an eyebrow, but ignored Ruth's dusting while she poured. "I don't think Grandpa suffered hardly any."

Ruth inspected her cup closely before taking a sip. "And that's a comfort. People were awfully nice. All those telegrams and the flowers. It was so sweet of everyone." She took a tentative sip.

"Don't be a fussbudget, Mama," Helen grumbled. "I washed the cups this morning."

Ruth rolled her eyes, a pink tinge of embarrassment on her cheeks. "Wasn't Grandma a pillar of strength? I was so proud of her." She gave a nod and murmur of approval after a long sip. "Good coffee."

Helen smiled. "Thank you. Yeah, Grandma held up really well. Is Aunt Flo Mae taking care of her?"

After another long sip to endorse Helen's housekeeping, Ruth leaned back in her chair. "Yes." She paused a moment. "But I don't know for how long."

"What do you mean?"

"Grandma went to the hospital last night. Came on suddenly, but she's improving. She's back home now. Had the flu."

"Oh, my Lord!"

Ruth nodded. "Yes, it came as a surprise. Flo can't be at her side every minute, so we had to hire a nurse, cook, and housekeeping help."

"What's gonna happen?"

"We can't afford the help for too long so I will want to stay with her until she gets her strength back."

Both women went quiet, lost in thought.

After another sip of coffee Ruth smiled. "Are you still seeing Preston?"

Helen gave Ruth a serious look. "Don't ask. Let's change the subject."

Ruth sighed. "Poor girl. So sorry." She looked at the ceiling. "He reminds me of Robert, in some way. You know?" She glanced at Helen. "Nice looking, on the quiet side –"

Helen gritted her teeth. "Ahem, speaking of disappointments, how are you and Ira getting along?"

Ruth set her cup down. She shifted in her seat and a cloud of annoyance spread across her furrowed brow. "We're getting along just fine." She shook her head. "Not that it's any business of yours, but Ira has been a comfort since your father died and I appreciate his sympathy and companionship."

Helen's eyebrows arched skyward. "I'm only askin' Mama. I don't mean to pry. Just curious is all."

"I know what you're thinkin'." Ruth forced a smile. "You and the boys don't approve, but you're wrong about Ira. He's concerned about me, nothing more."

"I'm glad, Mama. It's just…" Helen hesitated. "It's just we're worried about you, you know? Ira seems like a nice gentleman, but…"

Ruth drained her cup. She looked at Helen and nodded. "Let's change the subject again, shall we?"

Helen let out a sigh and refilled Ruth's cup. The cloud of anxiety lifted when Helen sat down. "Well, Lena Hayworth asked me where the boys were."

"Oh, I knew it would come up," Ruth replaced her annoyance with a smile. "I already told Georgia Irene they were visiting Sam in California, figuring she'd tell everyone else."

"Have you heard from them?"

Ruth stretched her legs. "No. And that's a concern of mine. It's been almost a month since they left. I don't have an address and I've a mind to ask Buck for Sam's address so's I can write him a letter."

Helen looked out the window again. The one that led to California. A trickle of woe collected under one eye and she wiped it quickly, avoiding Ruth's face. "Let me get some more coffee," she said.

"What's wrong, dearie?" Ruth leaned forward and set her cup in its saucer. "Is your throat bothering you?"

Helen shook her head. "It's so thoughtless of them to leave us in the dark." She picked up the coffee pot. "They know we're wondering, on the edge of worried. It's like they've made up their minds never to come back." Her gravelly voice gave in to another cough.

Ruth frowned when Helen coughed again. "Goodness, Ellie, that doesn't sound good at all. Promise me you'll see Doctor McCranels if that throat doesn't clear up soon."

"Yes Ma. Did you hear what I said about Robby and Les?"

"I did, and you know what? I've been thinking the same thing."

# Chapter 2

Helen rested her back on a stack of pillows, brushed her unkempt hair away from her face with her hands and stared at the ceiling light over her bed. As she often did, she thought about her brothers. *I wonder what they'd think if they saw me now*? An opened envelope, addressed to her, lay on top of the blanket in the space between her legs, along with an assortment of books, paper and art supplies. She touched her throat and felt the bandage that covered an incision. A quick swallow caused a stab of pain. The recovery ward at Central Texas Hospital was busy that morning with nurses all around her changing beds and attending to patients. Helen appreciated the distraction. *I'm gonna write Robby back on hospital stationery*, she told herself. *That'll get his attention.*

"Your Mama is coming to visit this morning," a nurse told her. "She called just a little while ago to make sure you were up." The nurse moved Helen's clutter to a bedside table and observed Helen with a steady gaze. "Can I help you to the bathroom before she comes?"

Helen shook her head. "I'm fine, thanks…" She paused, clearing her throat. "Could use a glass of water, though." It was hard to keep quiet, but Helen resisted the urge to say more. Her throat complained with every word.

The nurse smiled and handed Helen a glass of water from a cart. "You're going to get your first cup of warm broth and applesauce for breakfast."

"Oh, how ducky." Helen rolled her eyes. "Going to be skin and bones when I leave."

The nurse kept smiling as Helen raised the glass to her lips. "Don't gulp, take little sips."

Helen winced as the cold water bathed the inside of her ravaged throat. “I’m gonna finish the cover today,” she murmured after a slow swallow.

The nurse took the glass and cleared a place for it on Helen’s crowded bedside table. “Nurse Willingham praised you to the heavens at our staff meeting this morning. We all got a look at your handiwork and it’s beautiful!”

Helen beamed and picked out a sheet of blue construction paper from the table. Cutout photographs of the hospital, along with scenes from wards, portraits of patients and hospital staff, adorned a banner headline made from stencils of different colors, ‘Central Texas Hospital, Annual Report.’ Bluebells, birds, stars, and hearts decorated the margins.

Ruth appeared from behind the nurse. She leaned across the bed and hugged Helen. “You look awfully busy for having just had your tonsils removed.”

Helen snatched Robert’s envelope and tucked it behind her pillow. She gave her mother a cross look. “Don’t you ever believe my tonsils were out. They were full of pus. Had to take stitches.” Her voice barely audible, she pointed at her bandage and winced from the pain of talking.

Ruth patted her daughter’s arm. She hid a frown and sat on a visitor’s chair, examining Helen’s sallow complexion and tired eyes.

“Boy, it sure has been painful,” Helen sniffed. After a minute collecting herself, she smiled. “Everyone has been surely nice to me, though.”

Ruth slid her chair close to the bed in order to hear her better while investigating the papers on Helen’s bedside table. “It doesn’t appear as though your throat has sapped your strength any.”

Helen held up the decorated cover sheet. “The nurses are getting out an annual report for the hospital and they made me art editor!”

Ruth wiped away a tear. "I'm so proud of you, Ellie. You're so strong and talented too." She slid her chair back, reached into a satchel, and handed Helen a small box wrapped in colorful paper with a ribbon. "Here's a little something from Jessie Mae and me."

"Fer me?" Helen handed Ruth the cover sheet and held the package with both hands. "What beautiful wrapping," her raspy voice straining. She held the shiny wrapping in the light. "It's so pretty, I hate to open it."

"You've been such a good sport about having to get your tonsils out late and all," Ruth sighed. "I hope you'll forgive me."

Helen untied the ribbon, carefully removed the wrapping, and handed it to Ruth. "Oh Mama, they were ready to come out, plain and simple." She gave a muted squeal when a velvet-covered jewelry box appeared under the paper.

Ruth forced a smile. "It appears I got you and Robert mixed up. I remember taking one of you to doctor McCranels late one night, but I'd forgotten which one." Her smile wavered. "I'm so glad you got it taken care of in time. I wish I had –"

"Hush, Mama." Helen flashed a disapproving look at her mother. "Now don't go spoiling the moment." She cracked open the box, peeked in and sucked in a ragged breath.

Ruth chuckled. "Jessie Mae suggested we skip cards and flowers and go straight to jewelry."

A gold-braided necklace, highlighted with an emerald pendant, sparkled under the hospital lights. Helen gulped and removed the necklace. "Emerald! My birthstone! How sweet!" After handing the box to her mother, she used both hands and held it against her chest at the base of her neck. "How does it look?"

"Beautiful. And it'll look even nicer against your pretty skin once that bandage is removed."

Helen carefully leaned back against the pillows and sighed, the necklace balanced between the bottom of her bandage and the collar of her hospital gown. Her eyes fluttered and a cloud of weariness crossed her face. She gestured for Ruth to hand her the water glass. After a sip, Helen opened her eyes and handed the glass back to her mother. "I can hardly manage it all," she whispered. "The operation, bein' art editor, getting expensive gifts, and Robby's letter . . ." She paused to rest her throat."...It's almost too much excitement fer one girl missing her tonsils."

"Robert's letter?" Ruth scooted her chair close to Helen's bedside to hear her weak voice. "What did he have to say?"

Helen reached behind her pillow and grabbed the envelope. "Jessie Mae brought it to me. He can't wait for us to come..." her voice fading.

Ruth's eyebrows went up in surprise. "You don't say." She fidgeted with the jewelry box.

"I'm just dying to go." Helen got up on one elbow and cleared her throat. "How soon do you think you'll be able to go to California, Mama?"

"I don't rightly know when I can do something like that." Ruth nervously folded the wrapping paper. "I have a few things on my plate . . ."

"You're still seeing Ira? If I may ask?" Helen's strength drained while she stared at her mother.

Ruth hung her head, avoiding Helen's look. "That's all it is. He's helping me get back on my feet, you know. And..."

"I wonder how his biz is thriving, or if it is." Helen dropped back on her pillow and gasped. She inadvertently touched her bandage.

"He won't tell me anything, but I figure he's in a close place for money right now." Ruth slid her chair back and reached for the nearly empty glass of water. "Want another sip?"

Helen shook her head and reached for Ruth's extended hand, her eyes fluttering again, trying to stay in the conversation. "It's no secret he's milkin' you for every penny he can, Mama." Her voice broke and she coughed. "Robby and Les feel the same way."

Ruth held Helen's hand and kept her gaze downward. "It's not what you think..."

Helen let go of Ruth's hand and closed her eyes. "You musn't get melancholy," she whispered. "Not when it won't be long 'till you'll be with your two dear boys!"

* * *

A week later Helen was in her street clothes waiting in the hospital's reception room and talking to the duty nurse when Ruth came to pick her up. The bandage was still around her neck, adorned with the necklace strung prominently in front. At her feet was Helen's satchel of belongings. A bouquet of cut flowers in a glass vase sat on the counter next to her. "Aren't these beautiful?" Helen exclaimed, pointing at the vase when Ruth found her.

Helen's face was flushed, but her hair was made up nice. She'd lost weight and her wrinkled dress hung loosely around her shoulders and waist. Despite the bandage, her voice was clear.

Empty handed, Ruth hid a blush of embarrassment with a smile. "They most certainly are," was all she could think to say.

"The nurses wanted to thank me for the work I did puttin' their annual together. I told them I didn't need anything, 'cause it was more fun than work, but they insisted." Helen and the duty nurse shared a smile then Helen held up a small card. "The card says, 'Although we hope you never come back, we'd appreciate a visit now and then.'"

Ruth chuckled and carefully kissed her daughter on the cheek, taking care not to touch the bandage. "That's my daughter, she comes in a patient and leaves a celebrity."

"We miss her already," the nurse said and gave Helen a wink. "She'd make a wonderful nurse."

Helen frowned and shook her head. "I watched how hard those ladies work. They're all saints, Mama. Unlike yours truly, if you know what I mean." She waved to the duty nurse, picked up her satchel and headed toward the door behind Ruth. On their way out, Helen whispered, "I wouldn't be there a week before I'd slap one of those cry-baby patients up the side of their head."

Ruth nodded. "The Steves aren't known for their bedside manner."

The glare from a warm, late-summer sun made Helen squint and she put her free hand across her forehead. "I nearly forgot what outdoors is like," she said looking at the surroundings.

Holding the flowers in one hand, Ruth pointed with the other toward a line of automobiles sitting in a parking area. "Uncle Stan's waiting to drive you back to your apartment," she said. "You sure you don't want to rest up a coupla days at my place first? I can put you up –"

"No thanks, Mama. I'm about as rested as I want to be."

After a gruff hello and a few congratulatory words from her uncle Stan, Helen climbed into the passenger's seat while Ruth got in the back with Helen's things. "I thought you might be interested in Robert's latest letter." Ruth handed the envelope to Helen as Stan pulled out of the parking area.

Helen grabbed the envelope over her shoulder. "I hope he's ready for me to come out," she said. When she finished reading, Helen shook her head. "Tsk, tsk. Isn't he going to be surprised when he finds me at his doorstep?"

Stan let out a snort, but didn't say anything.

Ruth cleared her throat. "Don't you think it would be wise to let the boys get things sorted out before you come knockin'?"

"My Lord, I'd be waitin' 'til hell freezes over before Robert makes a decision," Helen quipped.

"I agree with you there." Stan smiled as he maneuvered through traffic.

Helen took a deep breath and turned to face her mother. "This hospital stay got me to thinking, Mama."

"Uh oh." Stan slid a quick look at his niece. "Here comes trouble."

"You hush." Helen faced forward, her arms folded across her chest. "Everybody gets a chance to grab the golden ring. Some take that chance, some don't, but it's there every time the carousel horse comes 'round. It's there for the taking." She touched her neck. "Bein' under the knife got my mind off silly things that don't deserve the time of day and made me concentrate on what's important, like me, fer instance. Every time that ring comes in my direction, I'm paying attention to things that don't matter. Know what I mean?"

"Sure I do," Ruth moderated her voice so she didn't sound preachy. "You're worried about life passing you by. Don't think you're the only one." Ruth's seat creaked as she braced herself while Stan braked for a slow-moving delivery truck. "We all want that ring, or wished we had grabbed it, more'n likely. But what makes you think California is your future? It's just another place, after all. As the sayin' goes, wherever you go…"

"I know. I know," Helen interrupted. But it's new and mysterious! Don't you see Mama? My brothers are there, and I have the means to go. Isn't that a good enough reason?"

Stan lifted his head, addressing Ruth. "Because she's young is more to the point."

"What do you mean, you have the means to go?" Ruth asked.

Helen hesitated. "Well, it just so happens two gal friends are leavin' for California around the middle of November." She turned again and faced Ruth.

"Huh?" Ruth leaned back in her seat, brows furrowed. "Leavin' for California? How?"

"Thelma's going to visit her cousin in Los Angeles. Nancy is accompanying her, and, because they know about Robbie and Les, they've invited me to come along. They're takin' Thelma's brother's Chrysler Roadster while he's… that is, ahem, he's incarcerated." Helen stared out the window while Ruth waited, and Stan drove in silence. "Don't ask," Helen said. "Thelma told me it's nothin' bad. Anyway, the Roadster's got room enough fer me, and I've decided to go with them."

The conversation kept up its strained silence while Stan parked in front of Helen's apartment.

After the automobile shuddered and died, Stan chuckled as he climbed out of the driver's seat. "She's got ya there, Ruth. No matter the circumstances, she's got a ride and a destination. What else do you need?"

"Oh, Mama," Helen said. "I'm just dying to go places and see things, aren't you?"

"Yes, but I'm not sure the boys are prepared for you or me to visit just yet."

"Oh pish posh." Helen opened the passenger door and hopped out. "I'll be fine sleeping in a closet if that's all they got. Or the bathtub even."

Ruth gulped. She waited in her seat for Helen to open her door. "Are you going to write to Robert about your plans?"

Helen shook her head as she grabbed the bouquet and helped Ruth out. "Nope. All he'll do is fuss and fume. I'll save him the anxiety and just show up. The surprise will do him good." Her eyes lit up. "I know little Leslie will be glad to see me!"

# Chapter 3

"Hey Robert! There's a woman on the phone, wants to talk to you." Robert's supervisor, Alfred Cooper, called out through his office window, high above the sorting room floor. Alfred gripped his phone's hand set and pointed at it with his free hand. "Don't tie it up too long. This is a business line, you know."

Robert looked around his sorting station to make sure Mister Cooper meant him. *A woman on the phone? For me?* When he recognized Helen's voice he nearly dropped the hand set. "Ellie? Is that you?" Robert stammered. He looked at the telephone with suspicion, like he was talking to someone from Mars.

"Hi big brother!" Helen exclaimed. "Mama gave me this here post office phone number. Hope I'm not interrupting any important mail calls."

"What on earth are you calling about? Is something the matter?" Judging by the clarity of the call, Robert had a sinking feeling it wasn't long distance.

"Why no. Nothing's wrong, Robby dear. I'm in Los Angeles! Got here just in time for lunch and I'm calling from a drug store called Chaffy's Corners, at the corner of Seventh Street and Alameda Street? It has the nicest soda fountain –"

"You're not supposed to be here!" Robert interrupted. "I told Mama that we were getting a place ready for *her*. You're supposed to come later." Robert gave his supervisor a guilty look. Alfred pretended not to notice.

"Well, I'm here now and I'm not turning around." Ellie gave up her sweet voice. "Mama can't come yet. She needs more time before she can leave Texas."

"Oh, my Lord." Robert looked at the clock on the office wall. "I can't stay on this phone any longer. Tell me where you are again?"

"Like I said. I'm at this here drugstore at the corner of Seventh Street and Alameda Street. It's called Chaffy's Corners. When can you come pick me up?"

"Get a magazine or something. I don't get off work until after six and it'll take a while to reach you."

"Well, that's no way to treat a lady, leaving her stranded in a strange city for hours," Helen huffed. "Where's Les?"

"He's at school, least that's where he was headed this morning."

"School?" Helen sighed. "I guess that leaves me high and dry. Sure are a lot of strange characters roamin' around these parts."

Helen hid her anxiety behind a tone of false bravado, but Robert knew his sister was out of her depth. He also knew it would be dark before he got to the drug store.

"Don't pay them any mind," Robert replied. "Just stay put and mind your own business. I'll see ya as soon as I can."

"Family problems?" Alfred said when Robert hung up and let out a long sigh. "The look on your face speaks a thousand words."

"My sister just showed up in town without warning," Robert replied. "She's sitting at a soda fountain lost and bewildered."

"She sounds like a real live wire," Alfred smiled. "You can arrange with Roscoe to get off early if you like. I guess she needs a pickup."

"Thanks, but she'll be all right." Robert toyed with the idea of arranging to leave early, but dismissed it with a shake of his head. *Let her cool her heels*, he thought. *Take some of the sass out of her.* "She has a habit of shooting first and aiming later," Robert said as he headed back to the sorting room. "It's what happens after I pick her up that I'm concerned about," he muttered to himself.

*At least she's close*, Robert thought as he lit out after work. It was dark when he got off the Red Car at 6th Street, and he was relieved to see the drug store was still open. Inside, Helen was holding court at the counter with the other fountain customers.

When he came through the door, she was talking to a middle-aged man slumped above a cup of coffee, his chin balanced precariously at the end of his upturned hand, looking like he was nursing a hangover. "Well, if you're from Kentucky then you must have heard about the Howser family. They're my mother's kin. They have a place near Hodgenville? That's just south of Elizabethtown? They've been there for generations."

"No ma'am I don't think I have," the man replied, his eyes barely open.

A familiar-looking carpetbag hung beneath the counter and another smaller tote sat next to a strawberry milk shake. Helen's clothes and accent stuck out from the rest of the patrons like a sore thumb. Even in quirky Los Angeles where anything was possible, people stared at Helen like she was an escapee from the circus.

*Am I that jaded already*? Robert wondered as he approached his sister from behind. *I wonder what people thought of me when I got here*. "Ahem," he said.

Helen spun around, hopped off her stool and grabbed Robert like a drowning victim before he could say a word.

"I sensed your presence the moment you came in the door," Helen gushed. "Boy, am I glad to see you."

"Is that the brother you've been talkin' about?" The hungover gentleman glanced at Robert, frowned, and resumed staring at his coffee.

"Shore is," Helen replied, beaming. "He's here to whisk me away to home sweet home, wherever that is." She collected her bags while Robert paid her tab. "Been nice talkin' to y'all," she said amid a chorus of goodbyes.

While Robert escorted her out the door, Helen clutched Robert's arm and held tight. He felt his sister's anxiety through her fingers.

"Strangest people I ever saw," she said. "Strange dress, strange manners; they don't seem to care a'tall about simple courtesies."

Robert led Helen across Alameda to the trolley stop. "Before we get into a discussion about Los Angeles wildlife, I'd like to know what got in your head to show up without even a word of warning?"

"I had an opportunity to catch a ride for practically nothin' and I took it." Helen stared at the shop windows and streetlights. "It sure is lit up. I've never seen so many lights all goin' on at once."

"How long you plan on staying?"

Helen hesitated. "I . . . Quite frankly, haven't given that much thought." She peeked at Robert and giggled. "Until my welcome wears out, I guess."

Robert grunted. "But Mama was supposed to come out first. You read my letter, didn't you?"

"I told you, Robby. Mama ain't ready to come to California any time soon, so I figured why should I wait?"

A bright, single headlight appeared two blocks ahead. "Here comes our ride," Robert said getting up from his seat and grabbing Helen's carpetbag. Get your things together."

Half asleep, Helen lurched up behind Robert with her tote. "Excuse me," she said as they squeezed into the line of waiting people. "I'm awfully sorry, he's my brother, you see. And I have to follow him or I'll get lost. I have only just arrived in your fair city."

“My, that’s a pretty scarf,” Helen exclaimed to a tired-looking lady wearing a long dark coat. The trolly stop’s lights picked up the woman’s bright red and yellow scarf that poked out the top button. The lady touched the scarf and smiled. “Why thank you, dear. How nice of you to say.” Helen took a breath, but before she could get out another word the woman disappeared in the crush of passengers.

When they found a seat, Helen stared at the crowd of sitting and standing passengers, a dazed look on her face. She leaned her head on Robert’s shoulder and fell asleep while the streetcar bumped its way along Broadway. A moist, foggy breeze came in through the open window and bathed Helen’s face as she nestled against Robert’s jacket, her hair tousled and a smile on her lips.

“Here we are little sister.” Robert nudged Helen as they approached their stop and she woke with a start, looking frantically in all directions. “Where are we? My goodness I was plumb sound asleep. Did I miss anything?”

“Lots. Come-on we’re a couple ‘a blocks from our place. It’s called a bungalow court. Funny little houses. We don’t have ‘em in Texas.” Helen flinched in surprise when Robert held her hand as they crossed a busy intersection. “Step lively,” he said. “Autos here don’t care much for pedestrians. Les should be home by now. ‘Course, he doesn’t know a thing about you bein’ here. That ought to come as a surprise.”

“Ha!” Helen beamed. “It’ll be fun seein’ the poor little devil beside himself with joy and excitement.”

“I wouldn’t be so sure about that,” Robert replied.

“I can’t find the mayonnaise,” Leslie said when Robert opened the front door. The single living room light barely illuminated the room. “It was in the ice box this morning.”

Helen rushed in, dropped her tote, and put her arms around Leslie. “Surprise!” she gushed. “Your sister has arrived!”

Leslie stood stock still, arms at his sides. "Well I'll be," he said. "What are you doing here?"

The awkward sensation of hugging someone who doesn't hug back gave Helen a chill. She let go of her brother and took an awkward step back. "Aren't you even glad to see me?"

"Well, sure," Leslie finally said. "I. . ." he looked at Robert and knotted his brow. "It's just. . . I didn't expect you so soon. I thought the plan was for Mama to come first."

"I told Mama she should come out first," Robert added. "And put the place in order, you know? We don't have room for you both so I thought she should…"

"Hells bells! It's me, your sister. I just got here. Can't you two do better than that?" Helen put her hand to her mouth. "What's happened to you?"

Chastened, Leslie gave up a smile and nodded. "Sorry, Ellie. It's been kinda hard."

Helen shook her head and folded her arms across her chest. "Too hard to give your long-lost sister a kiss hello? Or even a hug? How hard is that?" She took a deep breath. "I know I come unexpected, sorry for the intrusion, but I'm family, goldarn it. Mama isn't coming for a long spell, and I wasn't going to wait. And that's the story, so get used to it." She cocked her head to one side, staring at the two young men. "You both look different," she said. "I don't know what it is. It's not just me being here. It's like you're preoccupied, older maybe."

Leslie laughed. "He looks older, fer sure."

Helen frowned. "Not that. It's your eyes, both of you. I've never seen that look before. It's like I don't even know you anymore."

"Now, don't go melodramatic on us," Robert said. "'Course we're different, but we're just as thoughtless and insensitive as ever." He smiled, trying to ward off hostilities, but it sounded flat.

Helen reached into her carpetbag. “Well, I may be unexpected and uninvited, but I didn’t come empty handed.” She handed Robert and Leslie packages wrapped in newspaper. “Maybe some of Grandma’s pecan fudge will help us get reacquainted.”

As she handed out the treats, she surveyed the apartment. In the gloom, one doorway led to another dark room, a second doorway on the opposite side led to what appeared to be a kitchen and a third closed door led to who knows where. *Probably the bathroom*, she thought. A window over a sink let in faint streetlight.

“Now, can someone please offer the lady a chair? Or do Los Angelenos have a habit of sitting on the floor?”

Sitting in a circle, Robert and Leslie opened their packages with care and savored the sight and aroma of Grandma’s fudge. “It’s the front page of the Goldthwaite Eagle,” Robert said looking at the newsprint wrapping paper. He scanned the headlines while nibbling on one corner of his block of fudge. “It’s like two gifts in one. Lookie here, Joslin Meadows was elected to the Brownwood County school board. Don’t that beat all? I never thought she’d amount to anything besides barefoot and pregnant.”

Leslie chuckled while reading the sports page. “We got whipped by Waco again in the semi-finals. Nothing ever changes. Oh, my Lord, Stanley Cline got kicked off the team.”

Helen smiled. “Kinda homesick, huh?” She unfolded the Gazette’s editorial and personals page and took a bite of her fudge, ignoring what was to her old news. “Nothin’ like Grandma’s wrapping paper to break the ice. ‘Course, the fudge helps.” She feigned a surprised look and pointed at her sheet. “I bet you didn’t know while you were hustling your way to California that Lorna Farnsworth went to Wichita for a week to visit her aunt?”

Leslie and Robert smiled and licked their lips while they continued scanning the Goldthwaite Eagle. The surprise made Robert give his sister a second thought. *Maybe her bein' here ain't all bad*, he mused. *We could use some new blood.*

Helen put a hand on Leslie's arm. "What's this I hear about you goin' to school? Brownwood High started last month, you know. Mama was wondering when you were comin' back."

The chill returned and filled the room. Both boys retreated from Helen's question by turning away and searching within themselves for an answer.

Robert shifted in his seat. "We haven't decided about that –"

Leslie harrumphed and spoke over his brother. "I ain't goin' back, Ellie. I've made up my mind. I been to the high school here and Brownwood High don't hold a candle. I'd be stupid to go back." He chuckled to himself at his pun. "Stupid both ways."

Helen frowned. "No foolin'? Really? Mama's gonna have a fit!"

"I can't help that. As it is I gotta take eleventh grade over. . ." Leslie lowered his eyes. "On account of my Texas education. Can you believe that? They consider it remedial."

"Remedial? Oh, my Lord."

Robert smiled. "He's gonna have to work for the first time in his life."

"But I'll be smart as a whip when I graduate, and I aim to go to college after that." He glanced at Robert and Robert gave him a strained look back. "And Robby's gonna go to college too. Aren't ya?"

"Yeah. Just as soon as I earn my way out of your school expenses, rent and groceries."

Helen stood and stretched. She trailed off quiet for a minute. "Whew! That's enough excitement fer one sitting."

"By the way, Robert said, pointing toward a table near the closed door. "Bathroom's pretty small so that's where we keep our towels and stuff. And keep the noise down. We're paying rent for two occupants. If the landlord finds out we got an extra boarder he'll either jack up the rent or evict us."

Helen reached for her bag. "Yes Sir! Now, if you'll excuse me while I freshen up. What's fer dinner?"

"Dinner?" Robert and Leslie laughed.

* * *

Helen woke up the next morning alone in the bedroom. Morning light streamed in the apartment and the bungalow looked different from the cozy den she remembered from last night. Shadows had hidden the tiny space. Glasses and dishes, books, newspapers, and magazines filled corners that were dark last night. A hodgepodge of distressed furniture was strewn about with no thought given to purpose. A dresser filled the kitchen, its drawers open. A jumble of pots and pans and packages of foodstuff took the place of clothing. The mattress where she'd slept took up most of the bedroom; in the front room was a pile of clothing where the boys slept. A small walk-in closet across from the kitchenette was crammed full with books and an assortment of junk Helen couldn't identify.

"Jeez Louise," Helen sighed. "And I thought Jessie Mae and I were a mess."

A note, hastily written, lay on the top of the kitchen's dresser.

There's coffee in the sink, matches in the top drawer, milk in the icebox and Wheaties on the counter. Should be a bowl + spoon in one of the other drawers. Be nice if you'd clean up a bit. Maybe some dinner? Here's two dollars. The Ralphs Grocery is two blocks south on 3rd St. Say hello to Sam. He works there. We'll be home around 5. Key is by the door - lock up when you go out. Don't get lost! Oh yeah, be careful with the toilet - tends to overflow during the morning rush.

"Thank you, Robby," Helen shrugged, padding to the bathroom in her bathrobe and slippers. "Such a fountain of help and consideration."

Preston came to mind as she washed her face. Los Angeles water felt different. Slimy, oily, it clung to her fingers and her cheeks and wouldn't let go. *People drink this stuff*? she wondered. Peering in the mirror, behind her tired eyes she saw Preston coming up the stairs to her apartment in his white summer suit. A bouquet of bluebonnets in one hand, the banister in the another. Knuckles tight, his face down, watching each step, willing himself not to stumble or fall.

A baby's cry broke her concentration. "Let him go," she mumbled. "I'm in California now."

The Wheaties were unfulfilling and she didn't like heating leftover coffee, but the disappointing breakfast was forgotten by the view out the front room window. A patch of lush green lawn filled a courtyard. Surrounding the greenspace were identical small houses, spaced close together, each with a covered porch. Helen stepped outside. The yard was highlighted by a fountain. Beds of colorful flowers lined the yard amid the sounds of chirping birds, barking dogs, and laughing children. "A bungalow court? Well, I never." Beyond the courtyard, through an archway, the street hummed with traffic noise. "Hello Los Angeles," she said, admiring the sights and appreciating the contradictions. "Let's get acquainted."

The boys had talked about Sam last night, him working at the grocery five blocks away on Third Street, so, after grabbing a shopping bag and tucking the dollar bills in her purse, Helen took a deep breath and stepped into the yard. *It'll be a good way to get Preston off my mind.*

"I declare, I'm overdressed and underdressed at the same time," Helen exclaimed when she reached the sidewalk. The late morning sun was warmer than expected and she quickly felt uncomfortable under her trousers, shirt, and woolen sweater. The passers-by made her envious of their cool, colorful outfits. Standing under an awning, Helen smiled admiringly at the ranks of loose-fitting suits, dresses and skirts, cloche hats and T-strap shoes that passed her, but she got no smiles in return. *They think I'm a field hand.*

Maybe that's what she saw in her brothers' eyes last night. Both of them had become used to living in this strange land of plenty and they'd paid a price for the privilege; their innocence. Carefree was replaced with careworn. People moved around Helen like she was a snag in a river. After another block, her smile faded as the disinterest she felt around her manifested in furtive glances, whispers, and giggles. At the stoplight, a little girl standing next to her, one hand clutching her mother's, pointed at Helen. "See the funny lady," she said when the light turned green. The mother shushed her daughter and hurried into the street. "I hope I'm entertaining," Helen replied.

The Ralphs Grocery Store was at the next intersection and, low and behold, there he was, rinsing fruit stacked in the sidewalk stall at Third and Vermont.

"Hi cousin, remember me?" Helen kept her distance, not knowing what to expect.

Sam focused on the fruit, washing and sorting. "May I help you?"

"It's your cousin, Helen Steves."

Sam stopped, turned his head, and squinted. "Ellie?"

"Ruth's daughter? Sister to Les and Robby?" Helen curtsied for the fun of it. "The one and only."

"Well, I'll be." Sam wiped his wet hands on his apron, but before he could extend a polite handshake, Helen leaned into him and planted a kiss on his cheek.

Sam flinched and rubbed his cheek. "Robert never said nothin' 'bout you commin'. I thought Ruth was supposed to come next."

"That's always been your problem, Sam. You think too much."

"The devil you say," Sam laughed. "How'd you like a plum up your nose, smart aleck?" Sam grabbed a dark red Santa Rosa plum off the stall and held it menacingly close to Helen's face.

Helen laughed, grabbed the plum out of Sam's hand and took a bite. The abundant juice caught her by surprise as it dribbled down her chin. She sputtered, bent over, and wiped her mouth with the back of her hand.

"You got a napkin, boy? The lady could use a hand here."

Sam laughed again. "Helen Rose Steves. My, but it's good to see you!" He handed Helen his cleaning cloth. "Juicy, ain't they."

"Well, that's the best welcome I've had so far. I kid you not. Both my brothers would rather I disappear."

"You must have given Robert a start. He likes things to go orderly, you know."

"Isn't he the poor dear. But enough about them. Why don't you come by for a meal or somethin'?"

Customers walked among the produce stalls and Sam turned his attention towards a customer. "Looks like I better git back to work." He made a quick wave. "Come back again soon. My lunch break is at two o'clock.

Sam's abrupt departure surprised Helen, but she told herself not to get annoyed. Sam was not known for his social graces. Left on her own, Helen stared at the beautiful produce. Every tomato, carrot, pear, and banana carefully placed in their display cases, blemish free, at the peak of ripeness. *Any one of these critters would take first prize at the Brownwood County Fair,* she thought, picking a Red Delicious apple from a barrel and admiring its color and feel. She thought of Uncle Stan's pears, how much work they took and how few ever made it market; and even those couldn't compare with what she saw here. She felt self-conscious standing and ogling the merchandise; too intimidated to shop. *Can I ever get used to all this bounty*? she wondered. Unsure about what to do next, she left the store and continued walking down Vermont Street.

A hand pressed against her backside and she stiffened, but didn't stop walking, hoping it was a careless unintentional contact. She waited to hear an apology, but the hand stayed as she walked, its probing fingers flexing and pinching her. "Excuse me!" Helen stopped and twisted around, panic in her voice, breaking the cadence of the sidewalk's flow. Eyes wide in fright, she stared into faces behind her, all of them sullen eyed, betraying nothing as they recovered from the unexpected impediment and marched around her. "How dare you!" she shouted.

Humiliated, Helen sat on a bench at a trolley stop and hid her face in her hands as tears fell behind her fingers. She took a deep breath to compose herself, but a sob rose in her throat and broke free. "I'm not going to let some lousy SOB humiliate me," she said into her hands. After wiping her nose and face, Helen stood and collected her purse and shopping bag. *Mama would tell me to shake it off*, she thought. *Chin up, girl and don't let the SOBs get you down. Jessie Mae and Preston and Uncle Stan would say the same thing. This was no time for blubbering.* As she walked back to the grocery store Helen stared at the faces that passed her with as much of a blank look as she could muster, clutching her purse, keeping her comments to herself. *I'm one of them now*, she thought. *Pretend it never happened. Nobody wants to hear about your troubles.*

* * *

Sam appeared from behind a stack of crates full of 'Old Mission Brand' oranges. The crate labels were a brilliant palate of vibrant greens, blues and yellows depicting a sunset behind a lush orange grove. "Pretty as a picture, aren't they?" Sam leaned against the stack. Luscious-looking orange rinds bulged through the gaps.

Helen nodded, avoiding eye contact and giving away her anxiety. "I wonder if they taste as good as they look?"

Sam picked out an orange and held it in the sunlight. “Ralphs Grocery will cheerfully refund your money if you’re not completely satisfied.” Droplets sparkled as they rolled down the perfectly shaped fruit.

Helen hid her admiration by moving into another aisle. “Well, if looks ain’t deceiving they sure put Uncle Stan’s produce to shame, I’ll say that much.” She wanted to chat with her cousin, tease him about Texas and try again to invite him over, but she put that impulse aside and concentrated on shopping for tonight’s supper to keep from crying. *Another time. When I feel better.* Her hand trembled as she placed her items in front of the cashier.

“Say hi to your brothers for me,” Sam said as Helen stepped away from the cash register, her grocery bag heavy. She turned, smiled, but didn’t reply.

“I wish I could just keep on walkin’” Helen said on the return trip to her brothers’ apartment. “All the way back to Texas.” She fought back tears when she realized she had no means to pay for a return trip home. And even if she could scrape up bus fare, going to Texas with borrowed money would be a travesty. She would just be another burden for Mama. Jessie Mae had a new roommate, somebody Helen didn’t know. Where would she stay? On another couch again? Helen shuddered, thinking about the unwelcoming experiences she’d endured in the past. *I won’t show up anywhere empty-handed again.*

“Might as well make the best of what I got,” she said, opening the front door. “Make myself useful until something comes along.”

The smell of rice and beans and Canadian bacon filled the kitchen and adjoining room and while dinner simmered, Helen put her troubled feelings behind her by picking up after her brothers. “They’ll rue the day they let me put things away,” she chuckled while arranging cleaned, folded clothes into stacks lined up on the floor against a wall. “I’ll let them figure whose is whose.”

* * *

# Chapter 4

"Nothin.' But I ain't complainin'," Helen said one weekday evening after Leslie asked her if she was free the coming weekend. Robert was at work and Leslie had taken over the dinner table surrounded by open books and papers. Helen sat in the front room listening to 'The Adventures of Gracie' show on the radio.

"So you're complaining about nothing?" Leslie gave Helen a wry smile.

Helen got out of her chair and punched her brother in the shoulder. "Now don't go makin' fun. I don't complain much."

Weekends were usually quiet affairs for Helen. She and brother Leslie enjoyed each other's fun-loving companionship and when the opportunity presented itself, the two of them liked to take in late night boxing and wrestling matches at the Grand Olympic Auditorium, events Leslie's girlfriend Patsy was not fond of attending. Helen had gotten used to playing second fiddle to Patsy, she rationalized second fiddle was better than not playing at all. After the incident on Vermont Street, Helen controlled her discomfort in the company of strangers with a heightened sense of defense and a quiet reserve. The outgoing gentility of southern manners had no place in Los Angeles, and she had quickly learned to keep her friendly green eyes cast down, out of harm's way.

The Gracie Show cut to a commercial and Helen sighed. "If you're thinkin' of us going to the Henry Armstrong fight on Saturday I'm happy to go, but just the same I'm bored. No friends, no surprises, no. . . No excitement. That's it. I came to California lookin' fer excitement. Boxing matches are fun, but they aren't enough."

"What kind of excitement you lookin' for?"

"Oh, you know. Parades, dances. . . that sort a thing. Something besides grocery shopping, house cleaning and mending other people's clothes."

Leslie set a textbook down. "Well, I don't know about any parades, but don't make any plans for the weekend because you're comin' with me on Saturday."

"Huh? Where am I goin'?" Helen turned down the radio's volume.

Leslie got up from the table and stretched. "Our class is holding a dinner and dance at the Beverly Wilshire Hotel. Winter break starts next week and we're gonna celebrate. I'm on the entertainment committee and you can help out before the shindig gets underway." He pointed at Helen. "Your compensation is to accompany me to the dance, so you'll need to look respectable."

Helen stepped back and covered her mouth with both hands for a moment. "But I don't have anything at all to wear! All I got are two pair of jeans, you know that."

"Well," Leslie shook his head. "Go to Robinson's or someplace and get yourself one of those dresses like you see in the catalogues. Wear your jeans while we're decorating. You can change later in the ladies' lounge."

"Robinsons? Buy a dress?" She put a hand over her forehead and through her hair. "This is happening so sudden."

Leslie shrugged. "You'll need shoes too, and maybe a nice wrap. It's January, don't forget. We'll make up for it by eating beans all next month."

"But . . . I don't know." Helen gulped. "I don't know how to dance. I'll probably say something foolish or fall down and embarrass you."

"You won't be alone," Leslie chuckled. "Everybody'll be talkin' foolish and falling all over the place by the end of the party. You even get to wear a party hat."

Helen continued running her fingers through her hair. "My goodness," she muttered. "Saturday is only three days from now." She needed a shampoo and rinse, her nails were a fright, but a chance to attend a big high-society dance?

"It'll be exciting. Just like you wanted!"

"Okay little brother," Helen replied. "But only if you promise not to run off and abandon me with some drooling lecher with a party hat over his nose."

"Au contraire, big sister. You'll rub shoulders with sons and daughters of the rich and famous."

"Yeah, 'til my shoulders fall off."

The boys weren't home when Helen got back from shopping. After putting the little change that was left in the cookie jar, Helen gulped at the prospect of getting by with what was left until Robert's next pay day. *Robert's gonna explode*, she said to herself as she added up the bills. *But I didn't buy a single thing at full price so there's nothing to be ashamed about. At least the rent's been paid.*

"Fifteen dollars?" Robert exploded that evening when Helen disclosed the tally. "Are you crazy? It'll be wood shavings instead of beans for us. Can you still take it all back?" He looked at his watch. "The stores don't close for another hour."

Helen stiffened, remembering her family's tirades when wives would, on rare occasions, squander the family savings on useless trinkets that, according to their husbands, did nothing more than satisfy female vanity. It was always the worst possible time. The men would rail about lost opportunities to make wise investments in some boring farm implement. Robert may reject his uncles' opinions and lifestyles, but he was still their nephew, similar in many ways.

"I'm not taking anything back," Helen replied. She gave her brother a stern look of resistance. "More than half of what I spent came from my sewing money and I chipped in some dollars from what I brought with me from Texas. I only used three dollars of your Post Office money."

Robert dropped his gaze and sighed. "Don't you understand? We depend on every cent. It all adds up to not enough!" He glowered at Helen, empowered by his anger. "We're payin' rent for three now, remember? I'll never be able to keep this bungalow squandering our earnings on high fashion!"

Helen let out a sigh of despair when Leslie spoke up. "Can we at least see what high fashion looks like?"

Robert dropped into his favorite chair and didn't reply.

Leslie winked at his sister. "Go ahead. Give us a fashion show!"

Helen stepped out of the bedroom looking every inch the socialite in a light green bias-cut dress that seemed to float around her contours as she turned. "It's a style called empire line," she said. "The saleswoman said it's very popular these days. And because I bought them all together, I got a thirty percent savings on these matching shoes and jacket. Aren't they cute?"

Helen did another slow turn while Leslie and Robert watched from opposite ends of the room.

Robert grumbled, but nodded at his sister's comely appearance. He grabbed the newspaper to hide his reaction.

"It reminds me of the green dress Mama got me for my twelfth birthday," Helen snickered. "Only this one's not as dusty." Helen glanced at her brothers. "I think it's just as pretty, don't you?"

"It'll do," Leslie said after a minute of silence. "Nobody's gonna point and laugh."

Helen stopped and, hands on hips, rolled her eyes. "Well, that's a relief. Tell me what you think, Robby. You're being suspiciously quiet."

"You look fine, Ellie," Robert said from behind the Los Angeles Times. "Nice clothes become you, no arguing about that. What I'm wondering is where does all this lead? Mama used to say one thing leads to another." Robert dropped the newspaper to his lap with a dramatic kerfuffle and glared at Leslie. "Unless you can find a way to pay for them, any more high-toned soirees like this one are going to send us to the poor house."

Leslie growled back at his brother. "I agree the poor house won't improve our fortunes, but neither is sittin' here with our heads in the sand." He leaned back against the wall. "There's a difference between saving and pinching pennies, ya know."

Helen giggled while she slipped her new shoes off her bare feet. "And what's the difference - if I may ask?"

"Well . . ." Leslie stared at the ceiling. "Saving is a plan. Pinching pennies is an obsession."

Eyes wide, Helen held her breath anticipating a fight, but Robert resumed looking at the paper, accompanied with a harrumph.

Helen knew Leslie was right. When it came to finances and gratification, all Robert knew was work and putting work's rewards in the family cookie jar. That was supposed to be its own reward, but it never felt like one. Back in the day, Mama used to always have some treats and fun little extra things squirreled away no matter how little money she had for groceries and bills. The fact was, Robert didn't know how to spend. More to the point, he didn't know how to live.

As Helen stood, shoes in hand, Robert dropped the newspaper again, less dramatically this time. "No use crying over spilt milk." He gave

Helen a wink. "I expect you to put those expensive clothes to work by having a good time."

Helen sensed a cloud of tension lifting and dissipating like a lost vapor. What just happened? The hard feelings had been so pervasive she hardly noticed until just now when the atmosphere changed from hostile to amicable. *It has something to do with Leslie*, Helen thought. *He's a man now. Robert knows it.*

# Chapter 5

"Talk about a swank joint!" Helen exclaimed when a stern-faced doorman wearing a bright red jacket with brass buttons led her and Leslie through the Beverly Wilshire's front door. It was all gilt and cupids and Aubusson carpets. Cut glass chandeliers with their sparkling prisms caught and held a festive feeling that permeated a lobby filled with energetic, excited young people.

Leslie pointed at a corner piled with jackets and cast-off luggage. "Put your bag over there. We were lucky to get the place. The hotel is booked up nearly every day of the year, but fortunately we have a few folks whose parents pull a lot of weight in this town."

Massive Corinthian columns lined up in long ranks led into the de pths of the hotel's interior. A gentleman dressed in a tuxedo, hidden among large flower arrangements and overstuffed furniture, played Tommy Dorsey tunes on a grand piano. The lush green carpeting and wall hangings muffled the sounds of business going on in dimly lit corners to a monotone of whispers.

"This way," Leslie gestured through a pair of oak doors that lead into an immense ballroom. Palm trees set in huge terra cotta planters circled the room's perimeter.

Helen walked over to a planter that was as tall as her waist and put her hand up against the tree. "So, are these things real?"

"They're real all right." Leslie waved to somebody and the stranger, a young man with shaggy brown hair, beckoned Leslie. Leslie gave Helen a pat on the shoulder. "I don't know how healthy they are, Ellie, but that's somebody else's worry." With a distracted look, he gestured toward a cluster of young women dressed in work clothes standing near the stage. "Anyway, this is called the Coconut Grove for obvious reasons, and here's where you'll be decorating. Talk to those gals over there. Tell Amy you're my sister. Gotta run. See ya later."

* * *

"Amy?" Despite being alone and abandoned, Helen felt safe and let go of her fears, caught up in the festive mood. She got a few funny looks when her accent lapsed into too much country, but people enjoyed her bubbly enthusiasm and energy. Amy was temporarily detained, but Helen was quickly put to work hanging crepe paper. *Maybe Les is into something stayin' in school*, she remarked to herself. *People here are a lot nicer than the folks downtown.*

"How you doing up there?" came a voice while Helen hung off a step ladder stringing crape paper behind the band stand. Helen looked down into the concerned eyes of a young woman holding tight to strings of balloons that struggled to be set free. "I'm doin' fine," Helen replied. "Looks like you got your hands full."

The woman jerked the balloons up and down. "Everyone's gonna set 'em free at the end of the dance, but I could use some help right now tying one balloon to each table's flower vase. You about done?"

Helen nodded. "Yup, this is the last strand."

"Good. Can you help me with these darn things?"

When Helen reached the floor, the woman held out her free hand. "I'm Amy and you're Leslie's sister, Helen. Am I right?"

"Right as rain," Helen answered. She smiled, still surprised by the spontaneous way people got acquainted in this strange land.

When all the tables were festooned with brightly colored balloons, Amy led Helen to table filled with glasses of champagne. "Here's your reward," Amy said, handing Helen a glass.

"My lands!" Helen exclaimed. "I'm having so many firsts today." She gave her glass an approving nod. "I hope this won't be the last champagne I ever have."

Amy giggled and clinked her glass with Helen's. "Let's make a promise," she said. "We'll keep an eye on each other's flutes tonight, make sure they don't go empty."

Helen laughed. "Flute?" She gave the glass a close look. "Is champagne so special it has its own glass?"

"And it's a nice glass, don't you think?" Amy held hers up to the glistening chandeliers suspended high above them. Lines of bubbles sparkled as they made their way through the golden liquid. "Holds quite a lot of the good stuff."

Helen sipped her champagne, then studied her glass. "Flute, huh. Any relation to the piccolo?"

Amy covered her mouth to keep from dribbling as she laughed. "You're funny, Helen." She put an arm around Helen's shoulders. "Let's you and I have fun tonight."

The transition from decorating committee to party guest took place in a crowded lounge smelling of perfume, filled with every type of garment and undergarment imaginable and non-stop chattering. Amy had disappeared when Helen walked in and she felt alone and embarrassed among the semi-nude ladies, all of them seemingly close friends. She found her bag and, since there was no place to hide, took a deep breath and started to undress in full view of countless strangers. While Helen was untying her shoes, Amy appeared holding her champagne flute, still wearing her work clothes.

"I'm holding up my side of our bargain and you've already lost your champagne!" said Amy.

Helen pretended to be alarmed and pointed at a sink counter. "It was right there a minute ago. Some half-naked reveler made off with it."

"You don't say." Amy held out her flute and led Helen to a love seat piled high with clothing. "Well, here. Let's share mine and wait out this madness." She grabbed an armful of jeans and work shirts, piled them on another seat and sat. "This'll do. I can watch people change clothes all day."

Helen let out a sigh of relief and relaxed with her friend while all around them women stretched, grunted, pulled, painted, combed, and zipped.

"We'll get ready after the crowd leaves and have the place to ourselves. I'm sure all those handsome fellas out there will survive the wait." She lifted her flute. "Meanwhile, cheers!"

After the dance got underway, Helen lost Amy again but found Leslie sitting at a table in conversation with the shaggy-haired guy. She rapped her brother on the shoulder. "Les. Do you know a girl named Amy? I didn't catch her last name, but she told me –"

"What took you so long?" Leslie turned in his chair and interrupted. "We've been sittin' here lookin' like a coupla wallflowers." He looked good in his blue double-breasted suit with a knitted waistcoat and sporting his favorite bow tie. With a quick movement, Leslie stood and pointed at an empty seat between him and his partner.

Helen huffed and didn't move, annoyed at being interrupted.

"Pleased to meet you," The other fellow stood and offered his hand.

"Likewise." Helen took the man's hand, but focused on her brother. "That's just the point I'm tryin' to tell you, Les. You see, Amy told me –"

"Ellie, this is Bridge Slater, the only friend I got," Leslie interrupted again. "He's from Oklahoma but don't hold it against him."

Flustered, Helen finally looked at Bridge and smiled, still holding his hand. Bridge wasn't as tall as Leslie, a bit heavier, but with handsome proportions overall. He was wearing a beige linen jacket with matching trousers which gave him a sophisticated look.

"I like your suit. You don't look like you're from Oklahoma a'tall." Helen quipped as Bridge let go of her hand.

Bridge smiled and hid a blush by looking away and pulling Helen's chair away from the table. "I'll take that as a compliment. Sadly, it turns back into overalls and hip boots at midnight. I hope your gown lasts a little longer; it's beautiful. No wonder it took you so long."

"It was Amy's idea!" Helen snapped. "She convinced me to –"

Before she could get another word out, the orchestra started up with a blast of horns and the dance floor filled with couples. The first piece was Fletcher Henderson's 'Can You Take It' and after the first few bars the dancers created a frenzied sight of color and motion in time to the pulsing beat. While Helen settled into her seat, Leslie stepped away from the table. "I'm going to run to the bar while everyone is dancing and git us some drinks. Mind the table and shoo away the riffraff."

Helen and Bridge maintained a shy silence until Helen spotted a bottle of champagne at a neighboring table. "I hope he brings us back champagne," she said. "Amy and I had been enjoying a glass… I mean a flute, each since we finished decorating and it sure was good."

Bridge nodded in agreement. "I like champagne too, but I have to go easy on the stuff. I'm susceptible to its powers. What were you decorating?"

"I was helping out with crepe paper stringing." Helen pointed toward the bandstand. "That's my handiwork behind the orchestra." She glanced at Bridge to check if he was paying attention. "It's supposed to look like a sunset. . . sorta, anyways."

Bridge studied the bandstand through the whirling couples. "Yes, I see it. I see the rays streaming out from a setting sun. Nice work."

Helen beamed. "It took a lot of crepe paper and I had to get up on a teetery ladder, but it was fun, really."

Bridge returned his gaze toward Helen. "Are you an artist?"

"I like to draw, but I'm more interested in decorating and sewing. I hope to be a clothing designer someday."

Leslie appeared carrying three flutes sparkling in the glow of the orchestra lights. It was an awkward carry without a tray and Bridge jumped up to help him.

"Let me help you with that," Bridge said while passing one tall glass from Leslie's grip to Helen.

"Only one for you, Bridge," Leslie reminded his friend. "Remember your limits." Leslie held his glass in a toast and Helen stood with her male companions. "Let the games begin!" He downed his glass while Bridge and Helen each took generous sips.

"Amy told me champagne glasses are called flutes. I keep wanting to tell you about Amy, Les. You know her, right?"

Leslie looked puzzled. "Amy? Amy Goulding? Dark hair, 'bout your size, perky?"

"That's her."

"Her daddy is in the movie business," Bridge said while they all sat down. "He's a producer or director or something."

"Well, I think she's swell," Helen went on.

"I do too," Leslie said. But, unfortunately for her. . ." He winked at Helen, "I've got my eyes on another gal. Also perky."

Helen rolled her eyes. "Another perky one, eh?" She gave Bridge a conspiratorial glance over her half-empty flute and Bridge smiled back over his. "Do tell, mister Casanova."

Leslie stood and surveyed the ballroom. "She ought to be around here somewhere, name's Patsy."

It was Bridge's turn to roll his eyes. "Patsy? You can't be serious."

The band switched tempo with the mellow string and brass opening to Guy Lombardo's 'You're Driving Me Crazy.'

"I know this song," Helen said.

The dance floor thinned out. "I know it too," Bridge replied. "Guy Lombardo is one of my favorites. I heard that after Bob Crosby he's the second most popular bandleader in town."

Helen took another sip of her champagne, "Who's Guy Lombardo?"

Leslie waved at a boisterous crowd gathered around a table on the far side of the ballroom. There were too many people for the chairs and the overflow stood behind those seated; everyone laughing, drinking, and chattering, oblivious to the orchestra and dance floor. Bottles, glasses, and plates of deviled eggs, nuts, fruits, and cakes covered the table and people picked at the various plates indiscriminately. "She's over there," Leslie announced. "In the blue dress."

"I'm not surprised." Bridge frowned. "Really, Les. There's nothin' but trouble coming from that direction." He offered Helen his hand. "Would you care to dance?"

Leslie put both his hands on the back of Bridge's chair. "Bridge, my friend, where you see trouble, I see opportunity. Patsy and her friends may appear to be privileged and undisciplined, but I see something more. Something –"

Helen took Bridge's hand and scooted her chair back. "I can't see that it matters one way or the other." She smiled at Bridge. "I accept your invitation to dance, even though I don't know how."

Bridge stood, took a last sip and smiled at Helen. "Champagne courage, my dear." He pointed his nearly empty glass at Leslie. "We'll leave you to your own devices, my friend. Meanwhile, please allow me to escort your charming sister to the floor." He swirled the remaining golden liquid at the bottom of the flute and set it on the table. "As you can see, I'm still in control of my facilities, err... I mean faculties."

Helen giggled as she got up from her chair. She felt surprisingly comfortable holding hands with a stranger she'd met only minutes ago. As they approached the dance floor, she tugged on Bridge's shoulder and whispered in his ear. "Now, who is this mister Lombardo again?"

"Guy Lombardo and his band, The Royal Canadians. Guy has three brothers and a sister and they're all in the band."

Helen gave him a curious look. "Are you sure you're from Oklahoma?"

The dancers enveloped them into a swirling throng of movement and merriment. Helen gently placed one hand on Bridge's shoulder and Bridge lightly held her waist. "We better get movin'," he said. "Just follow me. The worst that can happen is we fall down and get laughed at." He stared into Helen's eyes and whispered, "right foot back then sideways then forward then sideways again. Don't look down. Just feel the music. That's right. You got it. Now, again."

Helen hummed along with the music to get her mind off being nervous. At first she gave in to Bridge's control, but after a few bars she followed the repeating tempo and moved under her own steam.

"You're a natural!" Bridge exclaimed. Just as she began to master the movement the music stopped. "Shall we try the next number?" Bridge asked as they stood brimming with the excitement of being together and being a part of the dance.

"You must have escaped from Oklahoma before the awkwardness set in," Helen quipped, breathless from the exercise and the thrill of Bridge's company.

The orchestra started up 'Stormy Weather' and Bridge gingerly wrapped his arm around Helen's waist and moved closer. "This here is a bit slower so we can dispense with the careful footwork."

Helen felt the heat coming off Bridge as they swayed gently to the soulful sound. She found it easy to follow Bridge around the floor in time to the music. A hint of cologne came from his warmth, and she hoped he was enjoying the dance as much as she was. "So, what's the story about this song, maestro?"

"Well, Cab Calloway wrote it and it's Ethel Waters' favorite."

"Ethel Waters?"

"She's a negro singer. Sings jazz and blues at the Cotton Club in New York City."

"Humm." Helen gave Bridge a skeptical look. "Are you making all this up?"

Bridge laughed and swung Helen in a twirl that put a shiver down her spine.

Helen enjoyed their repartee. It added to the dancing sensation and made her feel sophisticated. She wasn't just hanging on to some oaf and getting led around the floor; they were engaged in a light-hearted conversation while dancing, just like in the movies. The song ended all too soon.

As the last notes dissolved into the ballroom's high ceiling, they self-consciously let go of each other.

"No," Bridge went on, "Ethel Waters is very real and very talented. I love her voice."

Walking back to their table, Helen squealed in recognition. Sitting alone was her friend Amy who squealed back and held out her arms. Everyone's glasses were refilled.

"Girlfriend!" Amy gushed and grabbed Helen. "I lost you!" She held Helen's arm and smiled at Bridge. "I'll have you know just a little over an hour ago this brave girl was up on a very tall ladder pinning up crepe paper." She let go of Helen and pointed toward the band. "And there's her masterwork. Beautiful, wouldn't you say?"

Helen placed a hand on Bridge's shoulder. "Amy, may I introduce Bridge Slater?" She gave Amy a quick nod and smiled at Bridge. "Bridge? Amy Goulding. Amy's the entertainment chairman." Helen pretended to whisper into Amy's ear. "Bridge says he's from Oklahoma, but I don't believe him."

"I'm hopeless on a ladder," Bridge said. "Three rungs up and the dizziness sets in."

"I know what you mean, Bridge." Amy held up her glass and invited everyone to join her. "I prefer to get dizzy on solid ground and in good company, thank you."

The orchestra resumed with 'Mood Indigo' and couples moved toward the dance floor.

"I was looking for your brother," Amy said. "He's supposed to ask me to dance. The committee expects me to make a dramatic entry, you know." She winked at Helen. "But I can't find hide nor hair of the scoundrel."

Helen and Bridge pointed their flutes at the rowdy table. "He's looking for opportunities," Bridge said. "Among the privileged and undisciplined crowd."

Amy rolled her eyes. "I bet Patsy's behind that."

After an awkward moment, Amy got up from the table. Helen gave Amy an anxious look, eyebrows up, and gestured at Bridge. "Can I recommend my friend here? He's a great dancer."

Bridge blushed. "I'd be glad to to –"

"Oh, good gracious no," Amy interrupted before Bridge could finish. "You two are perfect together." She shrugged one shoulder and shook her head. "I have plenty of beaus waiting in the wings." She stepped away from the table and reached out her hand. "Nice to meet you, Bridge." After a polite handshake, she clutched Helen by the arm again.

"Let's keep in touch, Okay? I'll call you next week. I have Leslie's number." A moment later, she waved and disappeared into a crowd of revelers.

Helen took Bridge's arm to keep herself steady. Amy's unexpected gesture of friendship made her lightheaded. So much socializing in such a short amount to time was difficult to handle. "Les doesn't know what he's missing," she said.

"Boy, I'll say," Bridge replied. He looked at the orchestra which began another tune.

Helen followed Bridge's stare. "OK maestro, what's this one all about?"

"Night and Day. Written by Cole Porter. It's the number one hit this year. Fred Astaire sings it a lot."

"You don't say." Helen took another sip of champagne. She felt a gentle numbing sensation percolate up the back of her head.

"I saw him sing it in The Gay Divorcee when it played at the Paramount in April." Bridge beamed as he lifted his flute.

Leslie walked by in a crowd of spirited young men and women. He waved a finger at Bridge, but didn't stop. "Don't let him sweep you off your feet with his musicology, Ellie," he said. "He uses it to hide flaws that lay elsewhere in that dark personality of his."

Patsy walked next to Leslie. She laughed and blew a kiss in Helen's direction. "Hope you lovebirds are having fun!"

Bridge smiled back at his friend and whispered to Helen. "Did she say something?"

Helen rolled her eyes. "I can't fault Les for enjoying himself. It's just a shame he has to find it with that floozy. She gets my goose, if you know what I mean."

Bridge laughed. "In Oklahoma we'd say she sticks in your throat like a hair on a biscuit."

Helen giggled and grabbed Bridge's hand. "C'mon, Oklahoma. Let's dance."

After more dancing, a four-course dinner, speeches and accolades followed by more drinking, Helen was barely able to hold herself upright. "I'm plumb outa' my element, Bridge," she said as she stared down at an elaborate dessert made up of sponge cake, strawberries, caramel sauce, whipped cream and topped with a rum-soaked cracker shaped like a rabbit.

Amy stopped by their table and her contagious enthusiasm perked Helen up, but after she left, Helen felt a bout of nausea coming on and a panicky moment of helplessness. "Oh dear," she sighed. "I hate to be a bother, but I should get home soon. Do you see Les?"

Bridge stood and surveyed the banquet hall. The orchestra was playing Happy Days are Here Again. A few stalwarts were performing the Charleston on the dance floor. Some revelers were making motions to leave, but Leslie was nowhere to be found. Bridge gauged Helen's distressed face. "I don't want you to end this evening on a sour note. How about I take you home and I'll deal with your missing brother later? Worst thing that could happen is he yells at me for kidnapping you."

"Go ahead and kidnap me. I'll scream bloody murder if he sees us. Just for effect. I only hope I don't puke first."

Half an hour later Bridge was helping Helen to her front door. "Don't bother lookin' inside," Helen said when they reached the landing. "It's a functional little place but uninspiring."

"I enjoyed this evening and I hope it won't be our last." Bridge stood stiffly and held out his hand. "I didn't plan to go, but Leslie insisted. You've made me glad I did."

"That goes for me as well." Helen held Bridge's hand and she hesitated for a moment before turning away. "Thanks for the ride home."

The door opened and Robert peered out, squinting under the porch light. "Hello! I thought I heard voices. Can I help you? Leslie and Helen aren't home –"

"I'm here," Helen blurted, followed with a hiccup. She blushed, gave Bridge a quick, distressed look and covered her mouth. "Robert, this here is Bridge. Bridge Slater. Bridge was nice enough to drive me home when we couldn't find Les and I wasn't feeling hundred percent."

"You must be Helen's other brother Robert," Bridge replied. He glanced at Helen. "She's just a little hung over is all. Nothin' a good night sleep won't fix."

Helen blushed again, then giggled. "Guilty as charged. It was that fourth glass of champagne that came with the salad; with anchovies in it? My Lord. Just too many exotic drinks and grub for this country girl."

"Well thanks, Bridge," Robert said. "Care to come in? I have some coffee. . ."

Helen cringed and shook her head. "Another time. We've already been over this."

"Thanks for the invitation," Bridge said and stepped away from the door. "But right now I best catch up with Leslie before he calls out the Army and Navy."

Bridge walked toward his car, but Helen tarried at the threshold, waiting for Bridge to turn around. Robert ducked inside and disappeared.

When he got to the edge of the courtyard, Bridge turned. Helen gamely held herself up with one hand on the door handle and waved with the other. Her hair was disheveled, but her gown still looked lovely under the porch light.

"Don't be a stranger," was all she could say.

"I won't." Bridge waved back.

# Chapter 6

The annual Santa Ana winds started early in 1938 and by late summer they blew down from the high deserts, turning Los Angeles into a parched dry landscape and fostering an uneasy mood among Angelenos.

One blustery day in August, Robert brought home a letter from Ruth during his lunch break. “Letter from Mama,” he said, and placed the unopened envelope on the dinner table in the company of three empty soup bowls, a loaf of bread, saltine crackers, two apples and assorted utensils and sandwich makings. Helen stood over the stove heating a saucepan of Campbell’s tomato soup.

“Lunch is ready,” Helen shouted while serving soup. “Get it while you can!”

Robert took a seat and crushed some crackers into his steaming bowl.

Leslie sat wiping his wet hands on his trousers. “A letter from Mama? I figured she’d forgotten about us. What does she want?”

Robert blew carefully over a spoonful of soup and crushed crackers. “Don’t know. I haven’t read it yet.”

After returning the saucepan to the stove, Helen sat at the table, opened a jar of pickles, and pulled out a slice. “I hope she’s finally gonna come, but she probably wants us visit and to send her money.”

Leslie lay slices of ham and cheese on a piece of bread, snatched Helen’s pickle from her plate and folded the bread in half. He ducked to avoid Helen’s slap and took a quick bite. “I wonder if the riverbanks been washed away. Wouldn’t be the first time.”

Robert picked up a paring knife and cut an apple into portions. He examined the envelope while chewing on an apple slice. "She probably wants me to send her stamps."

Helen removed another pickle and glared at Leslie. "Don't touch it," she growled while collecting sandwich ingredients.

"She thinks stamps grow on trees," Robert grumbled between spoons of soup. "Just because I work at the post office –"

"Was there any other mail?" Leslie asked, putting cheese on a cracker.

"I didn't look in the mailbox. I brought this home from the post office."

Leslie looked at Helen and she shook her head. "I'm just the cook," she said. "Mail delivery is extra."

"Any more soup?" Robert asked.

Helen gave Robert an exasperated look. "Just read the darn letter, why don't ya?"

Robert sighed and put on his glasses. He cleared his throat. "My dear children," he began.

*I wish I could reach out with a long arm and big hand to pick each one of you up, lift you over the Rockies on over the plains farms and hills to this little spot. The river at my feet, willows o'er my head, a spray of butter-cups across my lap as I write makes me feel too full of everything to do anything but enjoy it and just lie back among the sunshine and flowers and look at the sky in the very laziest manner. Breakfast over, dishes washed, floors swept, I was off to my sweet old mother-nature's garden spot. The banks of "our" Colorado. If that turtle pokes his head out at me again I shoot a clod at him. Maybe he claims this bank too. The river banks are worried considerably, but we will get used to them. The old diving tree and swing are gone, gone and the place washed away. In that swimming hole a fisherman caught me a fine mess of fish last Sat. nite. And also plenty for himself and family.*

*By the way, I hear the faint echo of hammers and tobacco spitting, as some men are fixing the house, rain proof and patching it up a bit. I borrowed the work-men from Olli & Edna. The job will cost me $18.00 but nails, window-panes, et cetera will be very little so you can send me ten or twelve more dollars before long.*

*I don't rightly know when I'll be able to see you all, but I'm hoping for ways and means not too far in the future. Mama is bedridden now most all the time and can't be left alone for long. She can't piece quilts etc as she used to, does a few little turns if she wants. Headlines of the papers is all the reading she dares to on acct of her eyes being weak. I aim to stay with Mama a great part of the time. I do all the cooking & most of the housework. No cooperation, everybody too busy to think of doing anything much for me and I hate to make my wants known so I trust to luck & chance to get my errands run.*

*Don't you worry about me, though. I do hope you do not miss me too much. I miss all of your pleasant company greatly making me to resolve to treasure and promote it more in the future. At a great distance you three seem like Venus and (oh those others) shining brightly out over the blue Pacific. That is what you seem like to me.*

*I just had a nice snooze. The plum-thicket near the house is a great place for birds to roost at night and such a twittering you never heard about dusk. Sounds like thousands hunting a good place to roost and they surely must be chatting about everything and laughing and joking and an occasional trill of song – no foolin. Now this is that letter that brings you (I hope) a breath or glimpse of the good ole out-doors. Do you like it? Now how's about a long letter from each of you.*

*If any of you should come in October, pear-money will be coming in (maybe).*

*Love – write soon*

Leslie looked at his watch and scraped the last of his soup from the bottom of his bowl. "Long letter."

"Yeah," Robert replied.

Helen nodded. "Poor Grandma."

Leslie grunted while putting on his sport jacket. "It doesn't sound good."

Helen stood and clutched the back of her chair. "Mama told me she was gonna come. . . Now I'm not sure. She'll come, won't she?" Helen looked at Robert. "Don't you think so?"

Robert took another look at the letter then lay it on the table. He gave Helen a terse smile. "All depends on Grandma, I guess, and maybe that Ira guy."

Helen bit her lower lip and wrapped her arms around herself. "I feel so helpless and sad." She raised her voice as Leslie opened the front door. "Mama and me were going to help one another, ya know?"

"Mama wouldn't be much help," Leslie scoffed. "You two were always at loggerheads anyway. Wouldn't be long until –"

"You don't understand!" Helen shouted. "You guys don't care if she comes or not because you're so busy with your lives. And maybe if I were a guy I'd feel the same." She sniffed and blew her nose. "But I'm a gal and my world is a whole lot different than yours."

Leslie shook his head and stopped at the doorway. "Don't have a hissy fit, Ellie. No sense frettin' about it."

"That's easy enough for you to say, but I'm the one who's stuck alone in the house all day."

"What about Bridge?" Robert asked. "He sees you often."

Helen bristled. "Bridge is a nice friend and good company, but that's all it is. I miss Mama, that's the point I'm tryin' to make. Bridge ain't got nothing to do with that."

Leslie smiled. "Maybe Bridge would like to be something more than just good company."

"Don't go tellin' me how to handle my affairs, mister socialite, or I'll give you a few pointers about yours," Helen snapped, her face warming with frustration. She balled both hands into fists. "I'll decide who's a friend and who's something more."

"Sheesh!" Leslie muttered. "I was only trying to help."

"Cheer up, little sister," Robert said after Leslie shut the door behind him. "Write and tell Mama we miss her." He placed his and Leslie's bowl in the sink. "Tell her our garden misses her too. The tomato plants are lookin' poorly."

Helen glanced out the kitchen window at the line of withered tomatoes, corn stalks, potatoes and spinach plants that clung to life along the narrow stretch of tilled earth that boarded the bungalow. "That's not all that's lookin' poorly." Helen sniffed and blew her nose with a kerchief. "Where we gonna get ten dollars?"

Robert shook his head, then took a deep breath. "I'll send her the ten dollars," he sighed.

Helen stared at Ruth's letter. "Oh, Robby, I just don't know. What if she never comes . . . I feel so sorry for Grandma, but it doesn't feel right without Mama bein' with us." She folded her arms across her chest. "I don't know what to do…"

Robert frowned, an edge of frustration in his voice. "Grandma's one thing. That Ira character is the real problem, the gold-digger," Robert grumbled. "Doesn't have a penny to his name. What did Mama say? He was a friend from school?"

"Yeah. Apparently, he appeared at Mama's doorstep right after Daddy died, uninvited. Strange coincidence. She'd never talked about him before."

"Makes my blood boil. You know he won't be easily persuaded to let go of his sweet deal."

"I just hope Mama gets over him before he steals her blind. Uncle Stan says he spends a lot of time with her and spends all of her money to boot."

"He's a smooth operator, all right." Robert picked up the newspaper. "And all we got to go on is maybe she misses not takin' care of us." He shook his head. "And that's a big maybe." Robert turned away and headed toward the living room. "Now I'm gonna finish the paper."

Through the screen door, the sky was hazy with soot drifting in with the eastern winds. The yellow-filtered sun reminded Helen of Texas sandstorms. *If Mama's not comin' to California and the boys ain't going to Texas where does that leave me*? She thought. *Can I make a life here with... with Bridge*? Thoughts about Preston and Jessie Mae materialized, in a fanciful setting filled with Bluebonnets, Indian Paintbrush, Lantana, and the other myriad of wildflowers that made spring in Texas like no other place in the world. She missed the genteel Southern way of life. The courtesies, the friendliness and comfortable formalities, the pleasure that came from being with friends who had known her since she was a child. She turned and retreated to the bedroom. "Maybe," she sighed. "But couldn't I pay just a teensy visit?"

* * *

When Helen met Bridge at their favorite drugstore soda fountain, she couldn't sit still. While Bridge got their orders, Helen re-arranged the condiment jars, adjusted her silverware setting, and moved her water glass twice. Bridge gave up ignoring her agitation when Helen reached for the salt and pepper shakers. "What's bothering you?" he said.

"Oh, nothin'." Helen stuck her hands under the table. "Nothin' more than usual." She flashed Bridge a shy smile, placed one hand on the table and grabbed her cherry Coke. "Thanks for the Coke. Isn't it a nice day?"

It was a nice day; an unusual weather event for Los Angeles in September. A surprise rain the day before had dropped the temperature and cleared the haze out of the basin. The San Gabriel mountains stood out prominently along the northern horizon like they had stopped by for a surprise visit. Bridge leaned back in his chair, a skeptical look on his face.

"You're welcome and it most certainly is," he replied. "But you're in one of your moods. Something's afoot."

Helen looked out the store window, avoiding Bridge's stare. Her short bob cut swayed to her movement. She drummed her fingers on the glass during the intervening silence.

Bridge concentrated on his cup of coffee and waited.

When the silence became too much to bear, Helen re-crossed her legs and blew a puff of air, ruffling her bangs. "It's just that I kinda miss Mama." She took a long sip. "I was hopin' she'd be living with us by now, but she won't leave... Les and Robby don't seem to care. . . But I do. Not that it matters much."

"What do you have in mind?"

"Nothin' more clever than to pay her a visit." Helen sighed and rolled her eyes. "Sounds stupid, I know. I don't have the money for one thing."

Bridge's expression changed to serious. "Would there be more to your Texas agenda besides your Mama?"

"Maybe a coupla courtesy visits. My friend Jessie Mae for one."

"That's one of a coupla," Bridge interjected.

Helen drew in a deep breath. "Well, of course there's all manner of family to check on."

Bridge frowned and stared at his cup. "What about your gentleman friend, Preston McCall? Does he warrant a visit, I wonder?"

Bridge received a nervous giggle in response. "Why Bridge, you sound positively jealous." A light pink color appeared at the base of Helen's neck. "Preston, I'll have you know, may get an audience in the company of Jessie Mae, if it comes to that." She sighed and looked at the ceiling. "Now, don't you go worrin' your sweet little head off. This whole conversation is nothin' but hot air." Helen sighed. "I ain't goin' nowhere."

Eyebrows furrowed, Bridge finished his cup of coffee and slid the empty cup to the end of the table. "Maybe I am jealous. The question is of what? Preston or Texas?"

"Now don't get all serious." Helen finished her cherry Coke with a long slurp. "I have no intention to run off with either one." She slid her glass to the center of the table and smiled. Looking around the quiet eating area, Helen pushed her chair back and tapped Bridge on the shoulder. "Come on, Oklahoma. Time for a walk."

Bridge got up from the table, offered his arm and escorted her out the door. She held his arm with both hands.

After the winter dance they had become an affectionate couple and when the moment was right, Helen allowed mild petting, snuggling and chaste kisses, but she would take Bridge's advances no further. She appreciated his forbearance, knowing he was playing the long game, but she couldn't bring herself to commit.

Bridge had freed Helen from her dependence on her brothers and he gave her the keys to the city. With Bridge at her side, Los Angeles welcomed her in ways she could never have experienced alone. Neither of them were fond of formal social life. They preferred to engage in the city's abundance of attractions on their own. Their favorite places, like Santa Monica, Griffith Park, Venice, and the Grand Central Market were mixed with less glamorous hangouts on the edge of seediness that reminded them of their roots in small town rural America.

They walked aimlessly up Spring Street, saying little until Helen stopped in the shade of a grocery store's awning and pretended to admire the fruit on display. A cloud of animosity filled the space between the two. She folded her arms across her chest. "We need to talk," she said.

Bridge kept his eyes on the fruit display and held up an apple. "About what?"

"You, me, Preston, Texas, Oklahoma. . . all of that."

"That's a lot to talk about."

Helen glanced at the grocer who eyed them from behind a counter. "Let's start with you."

Bridge continued to stare at the display. A thin smile crossed his lips. "Yeah, what about me?"

"I'm very fond of you, Bridge. I enjoy our time together and I hope we can continue our friendship."

Bridge returned the apple and stepped back from the display, avoiding Helen's eyes. "Same here, only it seems I'm sharing your friendship with another one of your friends." He shoved his hands in his pockets. "And I'm uncomfortable with that."

"It's not like I'm seeing anyone else." Helen replied. She reached out toward Bridge, but Bridge moved back. "Preston is a thousand miles away."

"Doesn't matter. Maybe it would be better if he were here. Then at least I could size up the guy. See what makes him so special."

Helen shook her head. "Don't be silly." She paused a moment, then tried to make eye contact. "I can't change my life, Bridge. Preston is a friend, yes, but I wish I could assure you he isn't anyone you need to worry about."

"I'm not worried, I'm uncomfortable." Bridge looked up and down the street, giving Helen the cold shoulder. "You mind if we continue this conversation another time?" He pulled one hand out of his pocket and glanced at his watch. "I have an appointment."

"Sure." Helen bit her lip. "Run away. That always solves things."

"No different than running away to Texas."

"That's not fair!" Helen held back tears. "I want to see my Mama."

"And please give her my regards." Bridge nodded and stepped away. A minute later he was gone.

During that minute, while Helen watched him disappear, she stood motionless as people passed around her. She waited for something to happen, to make her cry or laugh, but all she felt was a numb feeling of sadness. *I'm just as careworn as my brothers*, she thought.

* * *

Robert came home that afternoon to find Helen sitting by herself on the sofa, her nose in a book, a sure sign of distress. Her collection of fan magazines was nowhere in sight. Helen made no effort to welcome Robert when he came through the door. "What's wrong?" Robert asked.

Helen sniffed. "Bridge and I had a quarrel."

"Let me guess. Was it about Preston or Texas or both?"

"Both."

Robert placed his empty Thermos bottle on the dinner table, hung up his jacket and sat in the armchair next to Helen. "You knew something like this would come to a head sooner or later."

After a long pause, Helen closed her book and wiped her eyes. "It's not like we're engaged. We're friends. Have been since the start. Why can't he be satisfied with friendship?"

Robert felt awkward hearing Helen's question, having more often been the recipient of her advice. He leaned forward in the chair, hands on knees. "Maybe Bridge has a different idea what friendship is supposed to mean. You know? Perhaps he hopes for a more serious relationship… that leads somewhere," Robert coughed, "ah… somewhere more serious."

"Well, he never told me." Helen stood and paced across the living room. "All the time we've been together I thought we were happy with one another, ya know? Now you're telling me he's been hiding other feelings?" She stood at her bedroom door. "All the time we've been together. . ." She sniffed again. "He's been lying to me?"

Robert got up, grabbed his Thermos bottle and stepped toward the kitchen. "Don't jump to conclusions." A noise from outside caught his attention and he paused. "Bridge is a good fellow. Don't sell him down the river too hastily." He looked out the screen door. "Here's Les."

Helen retreated into her room. "I will if he deserves it," she replied. "I don't care how good a fellow *you* think he is. *I'm* the victim here."

Leslie barged into the living room, the screen door slamming behind him. "Hi, I'm home!"

* * *

Helen sat on her bed with the door closed, clutching her favorite stuffed animal to her chest. Sourpuss, her toy cat, had been the only memento from childhood she had taken from her Texas home. Outside her room, her brothers gabbed about food, work, school, plans for the weekend… *Nothin' about Helen. Nothin' like 'where's Ellie?' or 'Is Ellie OK?' or anything. It's like I'm a ghost,* she thought, *'til I'm in the way.*

Later that evening after the boys had gone their separate ways, Helen took refuge in her rocking chair, a wicker-type that took up most of the front porch. Yesterday's beautiful weather had changed back to the hot, smoky October, typical for Los Angeles that time of year, but a breeze cooled the darkening skies.

Helen had found the chair abandoned in a vacant lot while on a walk with Bridge and she'd convinced Bridge, with Leslie's help, to rescue it. "It's like the one we had at the house in Brownwood. Remember? Before Daddy died?" She led the way while Bridge and Leslie lugged the chair up San Vicente Boulevard.

"I don't remember. I was two years old," Leslie replied in between grunts.

The chair became Helen's safe place. Whenever her life turned unsettling, she could depend on the rocking chair's gentle motion to smooth the rough edges. After the sun's last orange rays disappeared behind a hazy western sky, Helen lost track of time rocking herself to sleep. Her chin rested on her chest while Bridge, Grandma and her mother dominated her troubled feelings. *Darn it all*, she thought. *I'm the victim, again, of those close to me.*

A noise startled her awake. The sound of an automobile interrupted her nap. Automobiles crowded LA's thoroughfares during the day, but the residential streets were quiet after dinner hour. Helen opened one eye. The auto had stopped, idling in front of the bungalow court. Curious now, she opened the other eye. The low grumbling engine sound persisted. She lifted her head. *Was it Bridge*? The auto was hard to see in the dimly lit street, but Helen knew it wasn't his.

Bridge would never apologize. That was the way with men. They never conceded. It was always up to the woman to patch up unpleasant situations. *But he'll wait 'til hell freezes over before I beg for his forgiveness.*

The driver's side door opened and someone exited the auto. A man walked around to the passenger side, stopped, and leaned against the door, crossing his legs.

Helen caught her breath. He was dressed in a formal gray suit. The streetlight made his face and hands look pale, and his tall bearing gave him an aristocratic look. He leaned against the auto and lit a cigarette. After a long exhale the man stared at Helen. "Excuse me, doll," he said. "Mind if I smoke?" His voice was low, but the words were clear.

Helen gripped the rocker's handles and rose to her feet. She didn't know whether to reply or flee. *Where are those darn brothers when I need 'em*? She peered at the man, trying to place him. There was something familiar about him, *but what is it? He must know me*, she thought. Where had she seen him before?

The man took another puff then dropped the cigarette with a shower of sparks. He smiled and stepped toward the courtyard. "Trust your feelings," he said. "Remember what Reverend Renfro said..."

A wave of panic sent shivers down Helen's spine, and before the man could say another word, she scrambled inside and slammed the door. After locking it and attaching the security chain, Helen peeked out the front window. The man and the automobile were gone.

Helen turned on the radio to calm herself and walked around the house checking and locking windows. "Trust your feelings? What's that supposed to mean?"

The security chain rattled, followed by knocking at the front door. Helen gasped in fright. "Who's there?" she shouted.

"It's your brother, Robert. Why'd you lock the door?"

Helen rushed to the door and removed the chain. "Oh, Robby. I'm so glad you're home. I just had the most frightening experience!"

Looking annoyed, Robert entered the front room. “Huh? What kind of experience?” He dropped his jacket on the back of a chair.

“A stranger.” Helen took a deep breath. “He got out of an automobile and… and he approached me.”

Robert paused, looked at Helen and frowned. “Did he say anything?”

Helen nodded. “He wanted to know if he could smoke.”

“If he could smoke?”

“Yeah. He lit a cigarette and just stared at me. I didn’t know what to do. He might have been… Oh, I don’t know. I thought maybe… Maybe he knew me. But when he started coming up the walkway I got scared so I ran inside and locked the door.”

“Hmm.” Robert peeked out the window.

Helen trembled. “There was something strange about him, Robby. I got the heebie-jeebies.” She wrung her hands. “He told me to trust my feelings. He said… He said…” Helen dropped her eyes and shook her head. “Nothing, really. Never mind.”

“That’s odd. Sounds like some kind of kook.” Robert pursed his lips, brows furrowed. “You have to stay alert, Ellie. I wouldn’t spend a lot of time by yourself outside after dark. There are a lot of strange people in this town.” He looked toward the kitchen. “Anything to eat?”

Helen blocked Robert’s way toward the kitchen. “I hate it, Robby! I can’t even sit on my porch and enjoy a peaceful evening without being harassed by kooky strangers!” A wave of frustration and anger washed over her. “I’m serious! I feel trapped hiding from all this depravity.”

“Take it easy, Ellie. It probably won’t happen again.” Robert put his hand on Helen’s shoulder. “You’re still upset.”

“Upset? About what?”

"About Bridge."

Helen shook her head, and her eyes watered. "I'm not upset about Bridge, darn it. I'm upset about this place! California! Los Angeles! I don't want to spend the rest of my life looking over my shoulder every time I step outside!"

Robert dropped his hand. "Before you get too worked up, why don't you sleep on it? Maybe you'll feel differently in the morning."

"A night's sleep isn't going to change how I feel."

While Robert heated his dinner of leftovers, Helen retreated to the bedroom. Sitting on her cluttered bed, she tried to calm herself among her little world of distractions, but the mysterious stranger with the cigarette haunted her. *Who could it have been*? she wondered. *He must have been at Grandfather's burial because he mentioned Reverend Renfro... Is that why he looked familiar? How could that be? I saw everybody there and I don't remember...* Helen hugged Sourpuss and revisited her memory of the burial. Faces and snippets of conversations flitted in her mind. *What did Renfro say? Something about finding meaning in your life? I don't understand.* She shook her head to avoid thinking any further, thinking about something dreadful, something she didn't want to imagine.

"No!" she said and stood. "That's not possible!" She forced herself to look around her room and push a dreadful thought out of her mind. Her possessions filled every nook and cranny. The free-spirited young woman who came to California in the back seat of a friend's Chrysler Roadster was now burdened with more things than she could stuff in a steamer trunk. Things that meant nothing to her. "Finding meaning in your life," she said surveying her jumble of clothes, magazines, and knickknacks. "Where's the meaning in *my* life? Is this it?"

She was half-heartedly picking clothing off the bed when she caught sight of her cash box still sitting empty on her dresser.

The phone rang.

Robert stuck his head in the bedroom door. "It's for you."

"Hello?"

"Helen? It's Amy. Can we talk?"

"Amy! What a nice surprise. I've missed you!"

"That goes for me too. Sorry it's been so long, but spring semester kept me busy and then the past couple months my phone has been just ringing off the hook!"

"Really? Are those admirers of yours finally catching up with you?"

"No, silly. Ha ha. I only wish. The reason for all the calls is because people have been asking me to decorate parties for the holidays."

"Gee, Amy. That sounds super! You'll do great!"

"Not without you I won't."

"What?"

"They all want beautiful crepe paper designs like you did at the dance! They loved what you did. Don't you see? I need your help. Remember? I don't climb ladders?"

"My goodness… I don't know. I've been thinkin' about…"

"Stop thinking, girlfriend. This is the opportunity of a lifetime! It'll be so much fun to work together again, and I promise champagne!"

Helen looked at the handset and shook her head trying to think of something to say while her mind raced a mile a minute; Bridge, Texas, Preston, Jessie Mae, Mama, and now this.

Amy cleared her throat. "Ahem… something to do with Bridge?"

"No. Nothing like that. He and I have gone by the boards these days. It's just that… I don't know. This is kinda sudden."

"Something's gnawing on ya I can tell. Listen, just give me one chance. I got a project starting next week. It's a one-day job and you'll make ten dollars. No obligations after that. Whaddya say? I'll even pick you up and bring you home. That way we can catch up on our way there."

*Ten whole dollars*? Helen stopped thinking. The money cleared a hurdle that had blocked her way to Texas. *Opportunities, that's what California is all about. The land of opportunities, good and bad.* She drew a deep breath. "Okay," she half-whispered.

When Amy finished, Helen did her best to sound enthusiastic, and begged off any more conversation. *I'll make this opportunity work for me this time*, she told herself as she hung up and went back to the bedroom.

She knew it, now that there was a way. Texas, and Jessie Mae, and Preston, yes, even Preston was where her heart longed to be. Suddenly, it all made perfect sense. She would return to Texas. California could never take its place.

"Everything all right?" Robert asked from the kitchen.

"Fine as frog hair," Helen replied. Back in her room, a post card from Jessie Mae sat on the side table, showing Brownwood's stately First Methodist Church with its six white Dorian columns. *I still think everybody gets a chance to grab that golden ring*, Helen thought as she studied the photograph and re-read Jessie Mae's short message, encouraging her to come home. She dropped back onto her bed and kicked off her shoes. *I thought I could grab it in The Golden State... now I know better.*

www.ingramcontent.com/pod-product-compliance
Lightning Source LLC
Chambersburg PA
CBHW022202160726
48282CB00024B/291
*9789395131070*